BLUE BANNER
BIOGRAPHY

Lionel
MESSI

Khadija Ejaz

PUBLISHERS
P.O. Box 196
Hockessin, Delaware 19707
Visit us on the web: www.mitchelllane.com
Comments? Email us: mitchelllane@mitchelllane.com

Mitchell Lane
PUBLISHERS

Printing   1   2   3   4   5   6   7   8   9

Blue Banner Biographies

Library of Congress Cataloging-in-Publication Data applied for.
Ejaz, Khadija.
 Lionel Messi / by Khadija Ejaz.
    pages cm. — (Blue banner biographies)
 Includes bibliographical references and index.
 ISBN 978-1-61228-467-5 (library bound)
 1. Messi, Lionel, 1987—Juvenile literature. 2. Soccer players—Argentina—Biography—Juvenile literature. I. Title.
 GV942.7.M398E53 2014
 796.334092--dc23
 [B]   2013023038
 eBook ISBN: 9781612285245

ABOUT THE AUTHOR: Khadija Ejaz is an internationally published and translated poet and the author of several books. She was born in Lucknow, India; raised in Muscat, Oman; and also lived in Toronto, Canada, and New Delhi, India. Khadija now lives in the United States, where she earned her undergraduate and graduate degrees in information technology. She has also worked in broadcast journalism at New Delhi Television and dabbles in filmmaking and photography. For more about Khadija, visit her website at http://khadijaejaz.netfirms.com. "To Sonal, my husband, the Manchester United fan. May we dream long in this life together, in our own theatre of dreams."

PUBLISHER'S NOTE: The following story has been thoroughly researched, and to the best of our knowledge represents a true story. While every possible effort has been made to ensure accuracy, the publisher will not assume liability for damages caused by inaccuracies in the data and makes no warranty on the accuracy of the information contained herein. This story has not been authorized or endorsed by Lionel Messi.

Lionel Messi shoots to score during "Messi and Friends" versus "Neymar and the Rest of the World." The match was played at the National Stadium in Lima, Peru, on July 2, 2013.

THE BOY WHO COULDN'T GROW

*G*HD.

In 1998, those three letters stood between Lionel Andres Messi and his dream to become a professional soccer player. GHD stands for Growth Hormone Deficiency. It is a rare condition, affecting just one of every 20 million children, in which a gland at the base of the brain doesn't produce enough of the hormone necessary for growth. Messi was 11 years old but only four feet, two inches (1.27 meters) tall. That's about as tall as an eight-year-old should be.

Messi had always been smaller than other children his age, but that had never stopped him from playing soccer. People called him La Pulga, "The Flea," because he was so small. But the change that came over the quiet, shy boy on the soccer field was startling. The other players were almost always much bigger than he was, but he'd whiz around them with the ball and slip through their defenses.

Gentle little Leo was ferocious on the pitch. He loved the game and did not like losing. Everyone could see that he was special, that he had a lot of potential. Many people thought that he could be a great soccer player one day for

Young Lionel Messi. The future soccer star began to play with his brothers and cousins as soon as he could walk.

his native Argentina. In his country, soccer was religion, and the players were gods. And no god was more revered than the legendary Diego Maradona.

Great things seemed to be in store for The Flea if he continued to play. Maybe he would grow up to bring back the World Cup trophy to Argentina the way that Maradona had done. What an honor that would be!

But suddenly it looked like it would never happen.

Messi would now have to seek long-term treatment for GHD and take injections every day. But this treatment cost a

Lionel Messi with his father Jorge Horacio. The older Messi would go on to manage his son's professional career.

lot of money, around $1,000 per month. His family could not afford his treatment. His father worked at a steel factory, and his mother was a part-time cleaning lady and full-time wife and mother. His parents also had his brothers and his sister to take care of.

Argentina was going through a difficult time. It had never seemed to recover from the disaster of Guerra de las Malvinas (the Falklands War). Argentina had always claimed the British-controlled Falkland Islands (which they called the Malvinas) and had invaded them in 1982. But it had only taken the British about 10 weeks to defeat the Argentinean forces. The president of Argentina, General Leopoldo Galtieri, had had to step down after the war, but things had not improved for Argentina after the end of his military dictatorship. By 1998, the economy was in terrible shape. Inflation was high; everyday items like bread and milk had become very expensive. A large chunk of the population had fallen into poverty, even in Messi's home city of Rosario.

It seemed like the end of the road for the Messi boy and his dreams. His father had tried to get financial help from local soccer clubs in Rosario and even the River Plate soccer club from Buenos Aires to help pay for the treatment. But nobody wanted to spend so much money on a little boy. Without the hormone treatment, Messi would never grow up to become a healthy adult. He would never be strong enough to play for Argentina. He would never get to bring glory to his country the way Maradona had. It seemed like little Leo would always remain little.

Yet little Leo grew up to become a great soccer player in the world. Maradona has called him his successor. People still call him The Flea, but they also call him the Messiah.

They even call him Messi-dona.

BORN IN ROSARIO

On 24 June in '87
A year after Argentina became champions
A star was born, a new dream
The Golden Foot was born in Rosario.*

And so begins the Spanish song "El Pie de Oro Llego," which means "The Golden Foot Has Arrived." The song is about Lionel Messi and was written by Argentinian singer-songwriter El Tigre Ariel.

"Golden Foot" refers to Messi. It was adapted from "El Pibe de Oro," or "Golden Boy," which is Maradona's nickname. Widely regarded as one of the greatest soccer players of all time, Maradona led the Argentinian team to the World Cup championship in 1986 and won the Golden Ball trophy as the best player of the tournament. One of his goals in the tournament was voted as the Best Goal of the Century.

Messi's story begins the year after the World Cup triumph. He was born on June 24, 1987, in Rosario. His parents were Jorge Horacio Messi and Celia Maria Cuccittini Oliveria de Messi, and he had two older brothers, Rodrigo and Matias. The youngest member of the Messi family, Maria Sol, would be born in 1993.

The hospital that Messi was born in can still be found at 1249 Visasoro Street. The Garibaldi Hospital, where Rossi was born, is named for Giuseppe Garibaldi. He was an important 19th century Italian military and political figure. Garibaldi was popular in Rosario because, at the time the hospital was built, over 70 percent of the city's population was of Italian descent.

Rosario is a city of European immigrants. Messi's family is of Italian and Spanish descent. His paternal grandfather, Angelo Messi, had migrated to Argentina in 1883 from the Italian town of Porto Recanti. Over a million people call Rosario home; it is the third-largest city in Argentina. Che Guevara, a famous revolutionary, was also from Rosario.

> **Messi was born on June 24, 1987 in Rosario, Argentina. Messi's family is of Italian and Spanish descent.**

The year 1987 had not been a good one for Rosario. Democracy arrived in Argentina after a long period of military rule, but the people were unhappy, even angry, with the government. Demonstrations and riots frequently broke out in the streets. Two bombs exploded in Rosario the day Messi was born, one of them in the part of the city where his father worked. There were fifteen blasts across the country that day.

Two days after his birth, Messi was brought home. His father had built the two-story brick house for his family. Messi would grow up practicing his soccer kicks against the front gate of this house, much to the annoyance of his neighbors.

His family bought him his first team uniform—the black and red of the local soccer club Newell's Old Boys— for his first birthday. His first soccer ball was a gift when he turned three. He started joining his father and brothers for games in the streets soon afterward. "We were stunned when we saw what he could do," said Messi's father to author Luca Caioli in *Messi: The Inside Story of the Boy Who Became a Legend*. Messi would spend hours playing soccer

Five-year-old Lionel Messi (front row, second from left) smiles for the camera with his Grandoli team members. His father Jorge Horacio watches over them in his light blue jacket.

with his older brothers and cousins and come back home in tears if he had lost or if he felt that someone had cheated.

One day his grandmother Celia took him to watch the Grandoli children's team practicing. Celia asked the coach, Salvador Aparicio, if her grandson could play even though the other boys were larger and older. She told Aparicio that she would take him home if he started crying or was frightened. She didn't need to worry. As Aparicio recalled to Shlomo Papirblat of *Haaretz*, "It was amazing, the ball stuck to his foot and he left everyone behind; he was unstoppable." That was just the start. "When we would go to a game, people would pile in to see him," Aparicio told Luca Caioli. "When he got the ball, he destroyed it. He was unbelievable, they couldn't stop him. He scored four or five goals a game." In Messi's second year with Grandoli, his father took over as coach, and the team went on to win every match.

> "When he got the ball, he destroyed it. He was unbelievable, they couldn't stop him. He scored four or five goals a game," Aparicio told Luca Caioli.

CROSSROADS

Argentinians have always turned to their national soccer team during difficult times in their history. The team is called Albiceleste ("white and sky blue") because its uniform's colors are taken from the national flag. The country was under a bloody military rule when Messi's parents married in 1978, but soccer was so important to them as Argentineans that they organized their honeymoon around the Argentina–Brazil World Cup semi-final match in Rosario. Though that match ended in a 0–0 tie, Argentina went on to beat the Netherlands in the finals a few days later. Pandemonium erupted across the country as the people celebrated one of the few good things that had happened to them in those uncertain, violent times.

Newell's Old Boys is a famous soccer team from Rosario and was a Messi family favorite. Messi's father had played with Newell's from the age of 13 until his military service, and his two older sons had started playing for them from a very young age too. Soccer is like that—loyalties to teams (some of which are over a hundred years old) are often passed down through families.

In 1995, Messi moved to the Newell's children's team. He continued his stellar performance at his new club, scoring 100 goals in his first season. He became a regular during the first team's halftime breaks when he would be called on to entertain the crowd by performing tricks with the soccer ball. He was part of the La Maquina de la 87 ("Machine of 87"), a group of boys on the team who were all born in 1987 and who almost never lost a match.

Adrian Coria, ex-Newell's player, ex-coach of the youth teams, and assistant coach of the Paraguayan national team, remembers Messi as a young player. "When you saw him you would think: this kid can't play ball," he told Luca Caioli. "He's a dwarf, he's too fragile, too small. But

Lionel Messi (in the Argentinean blue and white) vies with Ecuador's Frickson Erazo during a FIFA World Cup Brazil 2014 South American qualifier soccer match in Quito, Ecuador, on June 11, 2013.

immediately you'd realize that he was born different, that he was a phenomenon and that he was going to be something impressive. Why? Because he was explosive, he had a command that I had never seen on a football pitch. He's Formula One, a Ferrari."

Messi's interest in soccer followed him to school. He was quiet and shy and used to sit in the back of the classroom. His favorite subjects were physical education and art, but he didn't like math or languages. During break time he would chase paper and plastic balls around an old tree in the school playground. Despite his small size, he used to play soccer with the older children in inter-school tournaments. He became a well-known youth soccer figure, but his teachers remember his humility despite all his medals and trophies.

Messi's parents remained worried about his height. They took him to Diego Schwarzstein, a Rosario physician, when he was 9 years old. Dr. Schwartzstein gave the youngster a series of tests and finally diagnosed him with GHD nearly a year later. The doctor came up with a hormone treatment program for him, which involved daily injections. At first his mother gave him the injections, but eventually Messi did them himself. "At first it scared him a little," Dr. Schwartzstein told Shlomo Papirblit. "I can't recall a child who isn't afraid to inject himself, and his hand shakes. But

> "At first it scared him a little," Dr. Schwartzstein told Shlomo Papirblit. "I can't recall a child who isn't afraid to inject himself, and his hand shakes. But with time he got used to it and it became a part of his daily routine."

with time he got used to it and it became a part of his daily routine."

The treatments proved effective and Messi began to grow. But paying for them soon became a problem. Messi's family was able to pay for them for a while with the help of his father's social security and his employer. When the payments stopped after Argentina underwent a financial crisis two years later, Messi's father turned to Newell's. The club agreed to help, but their payments were too irregular to be reliable. Messi's father approached other soccer clubs. Some expressed interest, but none of them wanted to get in trouble with Newell's. Nothing eventually came of it. Things were getting so difficult that the Messi family started thinking of migrating to Australia.

That is when FC Barcelona stepped in.

Lionel Messi and the man who discovered him. Carles Rexach knew there was something special about Messi when he first saw him play at the age of thirteen. He fought hard to recruit the young Argentinean into the Spanish soccer club FC Barcelona.

Goal! Lionel Messi raises his fist in triumph after scoring Barcelona's third goal from a free kick during a La Liga match. The match was played against Real Betis Balompie at the Camp Nou stadium in Barcelona, Spain, on May 5, 2013.

SPAIN BECKONS

*F*útbol Club Barcelona, also known as Barça and Blaugrana ("blue and claret"), is a professional soccer club based in Spain, and news had reached them about a talented young Argentinean boy who some said was like Maradona. Carles Rexach, technical advisor of Barça, heard about Messi through a series of contacts and decided to schedule trial matches for him in Spain.

The first trial was held on September 18, 2000, at the Miniestadi, the reserve and youth team stadium near the Camp Nou, the largest stadium in Europe and the home stadium of Barça. Messi had flown in with his father and had his picture taken at one of the gates of the stadium. He played his first trial match with boys his own age and scored six goals.

Rexach attended the second trial match on October 3, 2000, which Messi played with boys older than himself. The match had already begun by the time Rexach arrived, but he made his decision before he even sat down. Rexach told Luca Caioli that "to those who tell me that I was the one who discovered Messi, I always reply: if a Martian had seen him play, they would have realized that he was very special."

Rexach wanted to sign Messi immediately but had to spend time convincing the others at the club. Messi was too young, he was a foreigner who would not be able to play in the national league, and the club would have to help settle his whole family in Barcelona and pay for Messi's treatment.

Camp Nou is home to the European powerhouse, FC Barcelona. With more than 99,000 seats, it is the largest stadium in Europe. Camp Nou is Catalan for "New Field."

Rexach didn't give up, especially since other major clubs like Real Madrid had also shown interest in Messi. Rexach had personally promised to sign Messi at a meeting with Messi's representatives at a restaurant in Barcelona. He drafted an initial contract on a paper napkin and signed it himself. The official contract, though, was ready on January 8, 2001. It paid for a new house for the Messi family in Barcelona, the cost of their journey to Spain, and provided the father a job with the club. The key element, though, was continuing the hormone treatments. "From my experience, children who suffer from a similar deficiency and aren't treated remain very short, sometimes real dwarfs," Dr. Schwartzstein told Shlomo Papirblit. "I have no doubt that, without the treatment that caused him to grow, he would have had no opportunity to become the soccer player that he is today."

Thirteen-year-old Messi arrived in Barcelona with his family in February, 2001. They stayed at a hotel at first but soon moved to an apartment on Carlos III Avenue. Messi started school at the Joan XXII State School in the Les Corts neighbourhood near Camp Nou and started training at La Masia, the Barça youth academy.

Messi and his family arrived in Barcelona in February, 2001. After only five months, Lionel's mother and siblings decided to move back to Argentina.

Messi's first year in Barcelona was difficult. Only five months into his new life in Spain, his mother, brothers, and sister moved back to Argentina. "We were suffering," Messi told Luca Caioli. "I missed Matias, Rodrigo, my little sister, and my mother. I used to cry alone in my house so that my father wouldn't see."

Messi received his provisional player's license on March 6, 2001, but wasn't allowed to play on the first youth team because he was a foreigner. He had played his last match with Newell's in 2000, but the club took almost two years to complete his transfer to the Federación Española de Fútbol

(Spanish Football Federation). He had also arrived on the Spanish soccer scene during mid-season when teams had already been formed. He had to be content with the B team. He also suffered injuries that kept him out of many matches.

At least his hormone treatment was working. By 2003, Messi had shot up to five feet, four inches (1.62 meters) and was on the youth A team. Alex Garcia coached Messi in those days. "I moved him all over the pitch so that he could develop all his skills," he told Luca Caioli. "It was almost a given in the youth teams. So I played him as a midfielder, sometimes as a centre forward, or on the right or left wing. But he didn't like it. Within a few minutes, he would drift towards the center behind the strikers. You couldn't stop him."

Messi began to settle in and swiftly moved up the ranks from the youth division to the senior teams. He debuted with the Barça first team on November 16, 2003, and with the C team a few days later on November 29. In 2004, he debuted with the B team on March 6. Later that year, he made his league debut against RCD Espanyol on October 16. He scored his first senior goal for the club on May 1, 2005. Messi was only 17, and at the time, he held the record of being the youngest player to ever score a goal for Barça.

The records would keep coming.

> **Messi scored his first senior goal for the club on May 1, 2005. Messi was only 17, and at the time, he held the record of being the youngest player to ever score a goal for Barça.**

CHAPTER 5

FASTER, HIGHER, STRONGER

Messi had not been allowed to participate in the national leagues without Spanish citizenship, so on September 26, 2005, he was sworn in as a Spanish citizen after satisfying a two-year residency requirement. He has held dual Argentinean-Spanish citizenship ever since. Messi played his first home game in the Champions League the day after he gained Spanish citizenship and received a standing ovation from the crowd when he stepped onto the field.

But he remained an Argentinean at heart. He turned down an opportunity to play for the under-20 Spanish national team and debuted with the Argentinian national team at the age of 18 on August 17, 2005, in a match against Hungary. He also represented Argentina at the World Cup in 2006 and 2010 and helped his country win the gold medal at the 2008 Summer Olympics in Beijing, China.

But life had really changed for Messi after he played with the Argentinian national team's youth division in the 2005 World Youth Championship. He was the youngest player on the team, and not only had he helped win the final against Nigeria but was also named the best player

The heroes of Argentina work together–Lionel Messi and Diego Maradona, head coach of Argentina, celebrate after Argentina beat South Korea in the 2010 FIFA World Cup South Africa Group B match. The match was played at the Soccer City Stadium in Johannesburg, South Africa on June 17, 2010.

and highest goal-scorer of the match. People had started asking him for his autograph, and in Rosario, the media mobbed his house. The Argentinians had been waiting for someone to fill the gap that Maradona had left behind when he retired in 1987. It was becoming more and more evident that Messi might just be everything that Argentina had been waiting for.

All those comparisons with Maradona that had followed Messi throughout his life seemed to come full circle at the 2010 World Cup when Maradona became the coach of the national team. Maradona was impressed enough by Messi to make him team captain and give him the number 10 shirt that he used to wear. Messi had already scored a goal on April 18, 2007, during a Copa del Rey semi-final against Getafe CF that was very similar in strategy and timing to Maradona's 1986 Goal of the Century.

Messi had also inherited the number 10 jersey with Barça when the noted Brazilian player Ronaldinho left the club in 2008. With their new number 10, Barça went on to win the Champions League, La Liga, and Spanish Super Cup in 2009. In the same year, Messi scored his club's 5,000th league goal. He became the FIFA (International Federation of Association Football) World Player of the Year and won the Ballon d'Or award for the first time. He became the first-ever four-time winner when he received the same awards in 2010, 2011, and 2012. With Messi, Barça went on to win the La Liga and Spanish Super Cup in 2010 and 2011 and the Champions League in 2011. Messi had already scored his 100th goal for FC Barcelona on January 17, 2010, and played his 200th official match for the club on March 24 of the same year. By 2011, he had become the all-time single-season top scorer for FC Barcelona.

Messi's record-shattering streak continued into 2012 when he became the first player to score five goals in a Champions League match. He also became the highest goal-scorer for the club at 232 goals and broke another record by scoring 91 goals in club and international play in that year. "Nowadays in football everyone wants to be fast," Santiago Segurola, a journalist with the Spanish newspaper *Marca*, said, "but speed leads to collisions. Messi amazes me in the way that he knows how to make so many decisions at such high speed without getting it wrong."

Today, the little boy who couldn't grow is five feet, seven inches (1.69 meters) tall. In 2009, he started dating Antonella Roccuzzo, a young woman from Rosario whom he had known since he was a child. On November 2, 2012, the couple became parents to a baby boy named Thiago.

Children's issues are close to Messi's heart, since he was a child who went through difficult times himself. In 2007 he established the Leo Messi Foundation, which helps provide financial aid to sick children in Argentina. "I get excited every day that a child smiles when he thinks that there is hope, when I see him happy," he explains on the foundation's website. "And I will keep fighting to bring joy to children with the same force and intensity that I need to remain a footballer."

In 2010, he made a further step toward helping young people when he became a goodwill ambassador for UNICEF, an organization strongly supported by Barça. "I know there are a lot of children that have diseases, many that don't have an education, many that don't have good nutrition," he explained on the UNICEF website. "I am ready to do everything I can to help them in my collaboration with UNICEF."

In 2012, a Russian club offered Messi a three-year contract for over $40 million a year and matched Barça's buyout clause for Messi at over $330 million dollars, but Messi refused. He had no interest in leaving Barça. "They took a chance on me when I was thirteen," he told Luca Caioli. "I wanted to make it into the first team and I did. I wanted to win many titles with this team and I did. But I never forget that I am just one person, without the help of my team-mates I couldn't do anything."

Messi maintains strong ties to his family and his hometown in Argentina and stays in touch with the members of the "Machine of 87." Today, he is one of the

In 2012, a Russian club offered Messi a three-year contract for over $40 million a year and matched Barça's buyout clause for Messi at over $330 million dollars, but Messi refused. He had no interest in leaving Barça.

More than a champion—Lionel Messi meets a young boy during a charity visit at the Hospital del Mar in Barcelona, Spain, on January 5, 2012.

Lionel Messi holds up his European Footballer of the Year award, the Ballon d'Or, before a La Liga match between Barcelona and Espanyol at the Camp Nou stadium in Barcelona, Spain, on December 12, 2009. Ballon D'or means "Golden Ball."

world's richest athletes. He makes about $40 million every year, and half of that comes from brand endorsements.

Argentina still pins its 2014 World Cup hopes onto The Flea. Will Messi have to live up to Maradona's name once again? Mariano Bereznicki, a journalist for the Rosario newspaper *La Capital*, doesn't think Messi needs to be compared to anyone else anymore. Is Messi the next Maradona? "No," he told Luca Caioli, "he is the true Messi."

1987	Lionel Andres Messi is born in Rosario, Argentina, on June 24.
1992	Messi starts playing for the Rosario soccer club Grandoli.
1995	Messi starts playing for Newell's Old Boys in Rosario.
1998	Messi is diagnosed with Growth Hormone Deficiency.
2000	Messi plays trial matches with FC Barcelona in Spain.
2001	Messi signs a contract with FC Barcelona and moves to Spain.
2002	Messi's transfer to FC Barcelona from Newell's is completed.
2003	Messi debuts with the FC Barcelona first team on November 16.
2004	Messi makes his La Liga debut on October 16.
2005	Messi wins the FIFA World Youth Championship with the Argentinian national youth team; he gains Spanish citizenship.
2006	Messi plays for Argentina in the FIFA World Cup
2007	Messi establishes the Leo Messi Foundation.
2008	Messi helps Argentina win the gold medal in soccer at the Summer Olympics in Beijing
2009	FC Barcelona wins the Champions League, La Liga, and Spanish Super Cup with Messi; he wins FIFA World Player of the Year and Ballon d'Or award; he starts dating Antonella Roccuzzo.
2010	Messi participates in the FIFA World Cup under coach Maradona; he wins the Ballon d'Or award; he becomes goodwill ambassador for UNICEF.
2011	Messi wins the Ballon d'Or and UEFA Best Player in Europe awards.
2012	Messi sets the record by winning the Ballon d'Or for the fourth time in a row; his son Thiago is born on November 2.
2013	Messi becomes the youngest player to score 200 goals in La Liga.

Barcelona

Year	App	G	A
2004–05	8	1	0
2005–06	23	7	1
2006–07	34	17	2
2007–08	41	18	13
2008–09	51	38	16
2009–10	52	45	10
2010–11	55	50	21
2011–12	60	73	23
2012–13	50	60	14
Total	379	309	100

International

Year	App	G	A
2006–07	6	2	1
2007–08	4	2	1
2008–09	13	4	2
2009–10	12	4	1
2010–11	8	1	1
2011–12	13	4	4
2012–13	13	14	2
Total	69	31	12

App = Appearances, G = Goals, A = Assists

Crisfield, Deborah W. *The Everything Kids' Soccer Book*. Avon, Mass.: Adams Media, 2009.

Doeden, Matt. *The World's Greatest Soccer Players*. North Mankato, Minn.: Capstone Press, 2010.

Elzaurdia, Paco. *An Illustrated Guide to Soccer: A Game of Strength and Soul*. Broomall, Penn.: Mason Crest Publishers, 2013.

Jones, Jeremy V. *Champion Striker: The Lionel Messi Story*. Grand Rapids, Mich.: Zonderkidz, 2012.

Sosa, Carlos. *Superstars of Soccer: Argentina – Lionel Messi*. Broomall, Penn.: Mason Crest Publishers, 2013.

Works Consulted

_____. *Lionel Messi: An Unauthorized Biography*. Chicago: Belmont & Belcourt Biographies, 2012.

Caioli, Luca. *Messi: The Inside Story of the Boy Who Became a Legend*. London: Icon Books, 2012.

Donovan, Kate and David Koch. "Barcelona star Leo Messi is newest UNICEF Goodwill Ambassador." UNICEF, March 11, 2010.
http://www.unicef.org/infobycountry/spain_52997.html

Faccio, Leonardo. *Messi: A Biography*. New York: Anchor Books, 2012.

Lange, Dave. *Soccer Made in St. Louis: A History of the Game in America's First Soccer Capital*. St. Louis: Reedy Press, 2011.

Lebow, Jared. *All About Soccer*. New York: Newsweek Books, 1978.

Lionel Messi Statistics
http://espnfc.com/player/_/id/45843/lionel-messi?cc=5901

Lover, Stanley. *Official Soccer Rules Illustrated*. Chicago: Triumph Books, 2003.

Papirblat, Shlomo. "Growing paean." Haaretz, July 29, 2011.
http://www.haaretz.com/weekend/magazine/growing-paean-1.375938

On the Internet

Argentine Football Association
   http://www.afa.org.ar/
CIA: The World Factbook—Argentina
   https://www.cia.gov/library/publications/the-world-factbook/geos/ar.html
FC Barcelona
   http://www.fcbarcelona.com/
Leo Messi Foundation
   http://www.fundacionleomessi.org/
Leo Messi: Official Site
   http://www.leomessi.com/

INDEX